Cornerstones of Freedom

The Freedom Riders

Deborah Kent

CHILDRENS PRESS®

CHICAGO

Library of Congress Cataloging-in-Publication Data

Kent, Deborah
    The freedom riders / by Deborah Kent.
      p. cm. — (Cornerstones of freedom)
    ISBN 0-516-06662-5
    1. Afro-Americans—Civil rights—Southern States—
Juvenile literature. 2. Civil rights movements—
Southern States—History—20th century—Juvenile
literature. 3. Southern States—Race relations—Juvenile
literature. I. Title. II. Series.
E185.61.K378 1993   92-33424
                                                        CIP
                                                        AC

Crowds of people streamed in and out of the main bus station in Washington, D.C. It seemed to be a typical day for hundreds of travelers. But for thirteen people—seven of them black, six of them white—this day was far from ordinary. It was May 4, 1961. These thirteen men and women were setting out to challenge the segregationist laws that had existed in the South for nearly a hundred years. They were the vanguard of a revolution that would eventually crush an old order. History remembers them as the freedom riders.

Shortly after the Civil War, the defeated southern states had enacted a series of "Jim Crow" laws. The term *Jim Crow* comes from an obedient, uncomplaining black character popular in nineteenth-century minstrel shows. Jim Crow laws restricted the rights of black people and kept them segregated from whites. For example, blacks were required to ride in separate cars at the back of railroad trains. On buses, they had to sit at the rear and had to give up their seat whenever a white rider was left standing. Blacks had to use separate rest rooms, eat in separate

A segregated movie theater in Mississippi in the 1960s

Signs like this appeared in buses in the South before segregation was outlawed.

restaurants, drink at separate water fountains—even read at separate tables in public libraries. Blacks had no power to change the Jim Crow system, because other laws prohibited them from voting.

Then, in the 1950s, African Americans began to take action against these unfair laws. In 1955, Rosa Parks, a seamstress from Montgomery,

Alabama, was arrested for refusing to give up her seat on a bus to a white person. Her action inspired Montgomery's black citizens to boycott the city's bus system. Rather than take the bus, blacks organized car pools, walked, or stayed home. The boycott went on for more than a year. As a result, both the bus system and Montgomery's downtown businesses suffered huge financial losses. At last, the United States Supreme Court ruled that Alabama's state and local laws requiring segregation on buses were unconstitutional—and therefore illegal. Montgomery was ordered to desegregate its buses. A few years later, black college students began "sit-ins" at WHITES ONLY lunch counters in the South. These protesters sat quietly but resolutely at the counters until they were served or taken to jail.

Though small victories were being achieved in the struggle to end Jim Crow practices, for the most part, the Deep South continued to resist such changes. A 1946 Supreme Court decision had outlawed segregation on interstate railroads and buses. Another ruling, in 1960, made segregated facilities in bus and train terminals illegal. But in spite of these rulings, the Deep

A sit-in at a "whites-only" lunch counter in Atlanta in 1960

As this 1961 photo shows, most bus terminals in the South openly defied the 1960 Supreme Court ruling outlawing segregation in interstate terminals.

South refused to desegregate its facilities; it simply ignored the federal laws. Now, in 1961, the freedom riders were launching a fresh assault on the system that had kept Jim Crow alive for so long.

"We decided the way to do it was to have an interracial group ride through the South," freedom rider James Farmer later explained. "This was not civil disobedience really, because we would be merely doing what the Supreme Court said we had a right to do. . . . We felt we could count on the racists of the South to create a crisis so that the federal government would be compelled to enforce the law."

As the bus rolled south toward New Orleans, the trip's final destination, the freedom riders

Freedom riders boarding a bus during their journey through the South

openly defied Jim Crow practices. White passengers took seats in the rear, while black riders sat up front. Whenever they stopped at a bus terminal, the whites went to the COLORED washrooms and waiting areas, and the blacks used the facilities marked WHITES ONLY.

James Farmer, who organized and led the freedom riders, was the director of the Congress of Racial Equality (CORE). For twenty years, he had studied the philosophy and techniques of nonviolent protest. Nonviolent resistance had been used successfully by the great spiritual leader Mahatma Gandhi to help the people of

India throw off British rule in 1947. Farmer was one of many black leaders who hoped to use Gandhi's methods to win equal rights for African Americans. "We were told that the racists, the segregationists, would go to any extent to hold the line on segregation in interstate travel," Farmer said in an interview years later. "So when we began the ride I think all of us were prepared for as much violence as could be thrown at us. We were prepared for the possibility of death."

James Farmer

At first, as the Greyhound bus headed south, the freedom riders encountered little opposition. But in Rock Hill, South Carolina, a fistfight broke out as white teenagers tried to prevent the blacks from using "their" washrooms. The police

Freedom riders in the "white" waiting room of a southern bus station

quickly broke up the fight. Apart from that skirmish, the freedom riders met no violence as they crossed Virginia, the Carolinas, and Georgia.

In Atlanta, the travelers divided, boarding two separate buses. Their fear mounted as they approached the Alabama state line. Alabama and Mississippi were the most rigidly segregated states in the South; in both states, the Ku Klux Klan (KKK) held tremendous power. Klan members believed that the white race should reign supreme. African Americans who dared to question white authority were routinely beaten and even killed.

As the bus pulled into the station at Anniston, Alabama, a screaming crowd rushed forward.

A man sits in front of one of the freedom-rider buses to prevent it from leaving Anniston.

A fire bomb was hurled through a window of one of the buses after it was stalled by slashed tires outside of Anniston.

Klansmen seized the black freedom riders and flung them toward seats in the back. Flying stones shattered the windows. Someone began to slash the tires. The buses pulled back onto the highway and and tried to speed away.

Six miles beyond Anniston, the damaged tires forced one bus to a stop, and the mob caught up with it again. This time, someone hurled a fire bomb through a rear window. The bus filled with smoke. Choking and terrified, the passengers scrambled for the doors. As the last people jumped to the ground, the bus became engulfed in flames.

Though all the passengers escaped without serious injury, the bus was completely destroyed by fire.

The second bus drove on to Birmingham. That city had such a reputation for violence against blacks that many blacks called it "Bombingham." A mob surrounded the bus as it pulled into the Birmingham station. Men dragged the freedom riders to the pavement, battering them with clubs and lead pipes. One of the freedom riders, James Peck, had to have fifty stitches to close the gashes on his head. Another member of the group, William Barbee, received such severe head injuries that he remained paralyzed for the rest of his life.

Birmingham police chief Eugene "Bull" Connor was a notorious champion of white supremacy. He looked the other way and let the mob do as it pleased. Later, when asked why no police had arrived to intervene, he replied that it was Mother's Day. All of the men on the force were at home, having dinner with their mothers.

Bull Connor

With their pledge of nonviolence, the freedom riders were defenseless. They tried to flee. They attempted to protect one another with their bodies. But they did not lift a hand against their attackers. That night, television viewers across America saw the flailing clubs and the bloody faces of freedom riders who refused to return violence for violence.

After the attacks in Anniston and Birmingham, the freedom ride came to a halt. The bus companies refused to carry the freedom riders any further, arguing that they could not continue to put their vehicles in jeopardy. But civil-rights leaders feared that defeat would set a dangerous precedent. If the protesters appeared to give in to violence, the violence would go on and on.

Almost overnight, civil-rights activists in Nashville sent another group of freedom riders to Birmingham. Before their journey began, President John F. Kennedy sent John Seigenthaler, a Justice Department aide, to meet with Alabama governor John Patterson. Seigenthaler insisted that all passengers, black

John Seigenthaler

John Patterson

and white, must have equal access to interstate transportation. Later, he described the governor's reaction to reporters. "I'm going to tell you something!" Patterson had roared. "The people of this country are so tired of the mamby-pamby that's in Washington, it's a disgrace! There's nobody in the whole country that's got the spine to stand up to the niggers except me!"

Eventually, Governor Patterson reluctantly agreed to let state troopers escort a bus carrying freedom riders from Birmingham to Montgomery. There would even be a helicopter patrol watching from the sky. Yet when he explained the plan to the press, Patterson added, "We don't tolerate rabble-rousers and outside agitators."

On May 20, twenty-one freedom riders set out from Birmingham. Some of the original thirteen had returned, including a twenty-one-year-old black divinity student named John Lewis. The ninety-mile trip was remarkably peaceful. Some of the freedom riders even dozed in their seats.

But just as the bus reached Montgomery, the helicopter and the state troopers suddenly vanished. Years later, Lewis remembered arriving at the bus depot: "It was eerie, just a strange feeling. It was so quiet, so peaceful. Nothing. And the moment we started down the steps of that bus, there was an angry mob. People came out of nowhere—men, women, children with baseball

White men attacking a black freedom rider outside the Montgomery bus station on May 20

bats, clubs, chains. And there was no police official around. They just started beating people."

President Kennedy's aide, John Seigenthaler, pulled up in a car just as the attack began. He tried to assist a young black woman who was being struck by several whites. But when Seigenthaler urged her to escape into his car, she refused. "Mister, this is not your fight," she told him. "I'm nonviolent. Don't get hurt because of me." Moments later, someone struck Seigenthaler on the head with a lead pipe.

When the crowd dispersed at last, the parking lot looked like a battlefield. The pavement was spattered with blood. Seigenthaler and another man lay on the ground unconscious, and many

Freedom rider Jim Zwerg after the attack in Montgomery

more people were cut and dazed. Nearly a half hour passed before help arrived.

The next evening, Dr. Martin Luther King, Jr., flew to Montgomery. A Baptist minister from Atlanta, Dr. King was the most prominent and widely respected leader in the civil-rights movement. He was a gifted speaker who had won thousands of Americans to the civil-rights cause, and he was deeply committed to the principle of nonviolence.

Federal marshalls stood outside as King addressed a rally at Montgomery's First Baptist Church. As he spoke of freedom and equality, another angry mob gathered. The mob

On the night of May 21, hundreds of people attending a rally at Montgomery's First Baptist Church were trapped inside for hours after an angry mob surrounded the church.

The Evening Star

WITH SUNDAY MORNING EDITION

Metropolitan Edition

New York Markets, Page A-19

109th Year. No. 142. Phone LI. 3-5000   WASHINGTON, D. C., MONDAY, MAY 22, 1961—44 PAGES   Home Delivered: Daily and Sunday, per month, 2.25   10 Cents

Alabama City Under Martial Law

Move to Boost District Police Gains Support

But Senator Morse Defends Mallory, Durham Decisions

By JOHN McKELWAY
Star Staff Writer

Legislation increasing the District Police Force to 3,000 men gained strong support today as the Senate District Committee opened hearings on local crime.

But enforcement officers who have asked for other legislation modifying court decisions which, they feel, are confusing and hamper their efforts at crime prevention, ran into a stone wall in the form of Senator Morse, Democrat of Oregon.

Senator Morse said he would support a 3,000 man force, recommended today by Senator Bible, Democrat of Nevada, who is chairman of the full committee.

But the Oregonian told members of the District Law Enforcement Council, called to testify today, that the Mallory Rule is as sound today as when it was written.

Mallory Rule Defended

The Mallory Rule makes a voluntary confession inadmissable as evidence if there was unnecessary delay between arrest and arraignment. The council has asked that the ruling be clarified.

"Don't tell me," Senator Morse said, "you can't have an effective police force without police state methods."

The Senator called the Mallory Rule a "great decision" and said a suspect is entitled to

Cuban Rebels Fly Here To Begin Ransom Talks

Prisoners and Their U. S. Benefactors To Discuss Castro Exchange Proposal

By the Associated Press

Cuban rebels arranged a meeting with their American benefactors today to discuss Fidel Castro's ransom terms for 1,214 men captured in the Cuban invasion failure.

Mrs. Eleanor Roosevelt, Dr. Milton Eisenhower and Union Leader Walter Reuther head a drive to raise millions of dollars to purchase 500 American tractors or bulldozers demanded by the Cuban Prime Minister in exchange for the consideration" to granting export licenses if the tractors are purchased by private funds.

Mrs. Roosevelt is the widow of President Franklin D. Roosevelt; Dr. Eisenhower is president of Johns Hopkins University and brother of former President Dwight D. Eisenhower; Mr. Reuther is president of the United Automobile Workers Union.

They were scheduled to meet today with the 10 representatives of the prisoners; Dr. Jose Miro Cardona, chairman of the Cuban Revolutionary Council, and council member Antonio de Varona. The 10 representatives were paroled by the Cuban government to work out arrangements to free them and their companions.

Dr. Miro Cardona has been in bed with pneumonia but a spokesman at his home said the exile leader has recovered sufficiently to make the trip.

The Cubans were flying here from Miami, Fla.

The sons of both Dr. Miro Cardona and Mr. De Varona are among the prisoners held by Mr. Castro.

Spare Parts Demanded

Ulises Carbo, spokesman for the prisoners' representatives, said Mr. Castro had specified international Harvester or Caterpillar heavy tractors. He declined comment on a report Mr. Castro also demanded a large supply of spare parts and a five-

South Korean Government Reported Split

Military Leaders Disagree Over Power Division

SEOUL, May 22 (AP)—A split was reported in South Korea's new military government today over the division of power among the military services.

A competent source said marines and paratroopers who took over Seoul last Tuesday are the shock troops of the coup refused an order Saturday to withdraw from the capitol building and return to their camps outside Seoul.

The marines and paratroopers demanded more places on the 30-member revolutionary council, which except for a marine brigadier general and colonel consists entirely of army officers. There is also a marine colonel in the cabinet of 15 officers that was sworn in yesterday.

Demand by Magruder

United States Gen. Carter B. Magruder, under whose United Nations command all South Korean forces are placed, reportedly demanded Saturday that all the 3,600 troops used in the coup return to their original stations.

The order to move out was issued by Lt. Gen. Chang Do-young, the junta chief who also is premier, defense minister and army chief of staff.

Although the marines and paratroopers furnished the troops for the coup, the composition of the revolutionary council and the cabinet reflected the relative strength of

Governor Acts After Mob Battles Marshals, Police

U. S. Warned To Stay Out Of Race Fight

By CECIL HOLLAND
Star Staff Writer

MONTGOMERY, Ala., May 22.—A rampaging mob which besieged about 1,000 Negroes attending a church meeting, overturned automobiles and set them afire, smashed windows and hurled fire bombs brought martial rule to this Deep South city today.

Gov. John Patterson signed the emergency order last night as city police, State patrolmen and United States marshals battled the mob with repeated rounds of tear gas, clubs and, in the end, some warning pistol shots.

When the mob—estimated at 800 or more— was dispersed, small gangs roving through the streets of this one-time capital of the Confederacy led Alabama officials to insist on the Negroes remaining in the church for most of the night for their own safety.

Negroes Get Guards

It was not until 3:15 a.m. (CST) that the Negroes were allowed to leave the church. They were taken to their homes guarded by troopers with rifles and fixed bayonets.

Four hours during the night, police cars, motorcycle officers, deputy sheriffs and Federal marshals, sent here over Gov. Patterson's bitter protest

National Guardsmen fasten the tailgate of a military truck as they begin taking Negroes home from a beleaguered church in Montgomery, Ala., early today.—AP Wirephoto.

---

surrounded the church, trapping King and hundreds of his supporters inside. As the hours passed, their terror mounted. If the marshalls could not control the mob, someone might set fire to the church, and they would all perish in the blaze. To stem the rising panic, King quoted a song that had become the anthem of the civil-rights movement. "We are not afraid," he told the crowd in the church. "And we shall overcome!"

Finally, Attorney General Robert Kennedy ordered Governor Patterson to declare martial law in Alabama. State police and the Alabama National Guard helped the federal marshalls break up the mob. At 4:00 A.M., King and the others were free to leave the church.

The next day, newspapers all over the nation reported how National Guardsmen were sent to Montgomery– despite bitter protests by Alabama's governor– to restore order and escort home safely those who had been trapped inside the church.

Undaunted by the earlier violence, a new group of freedom riders, shielded by National Guardsmen, arrived in Montgomery on May 24.

National Guardsmen on duty in Montgomery

The freedom ride was still not over. On May 27, more than three weeks after the first bus had left Washington, twenty-seven freedom riders boarded a bus in Montgomery. As James Farmer glanced down the rows of seats, he noticed that many of the young men and women were feverishly writing farewell notes to their parents, brothers, and sisters. This would be the most perilous leg of the journey. In Mississippi, they would truly be on enemy soil.

Yet this time, there was no bloodshed. Instead of a raging mob, dozens of uniformed policemen waited at the bus terminal in Jackson,

Freedom riders being arrested for using the "whites only" waiting room at the Jackson, Mississippi, bus terminal

Mississippi. With chilling efficiency, the officers herded the freedom riders through the WHITES ONLY waiting room and into paddy wagons outside. Before they even knew what was happening, the freedom riders were arrested for breaking state segregation laws. The next day they were tried and sentenced to sixty days in the state penitentiary.

The freedom riders never reached New Orleans. But their courage and dedication inspired thousands of other Americans. Over the next four years, wave after wave of men and women—black and white, young and old—swept into the South to work with the civil-rights movement. Some helped African Americans register to vote. Others taught farm workers to read and write. Still others introduced children to African-American history, or marched to protest political injustice. Wherever they went, they were known as freedom riders.

After the first freedom rides of 1961, civil-rights leaders shifted their concerns from the integration of public facilities to a quest for political power. Unless they could vote, African Americans would never be first-class citizens. Once they won the power of the ballot, elected officials would have to respond to their needs.

For nearly a century, literacy tests and other laws in the southern states had made most black

As the civil rights movement gained momentum, its focus shifted to ending discrimination in voting, housing, schooling, and employment.

A nineteenth-century political cartoon criticizing the South's use of literacy tests to prevent blacks from voting

people ineligible to vote in local or national elections. To vote in Mississippi, for example, it was necessary to fill out a lengthy form. It included such questions as: "Interpret any of the 286 sections of the Mississippi Constitution to the satisfaction of the registrar." The registrars (invariably white) were seldom satisfied with the answers given by black applicants. Forty-five percent of all Mississippians were black, but only five percent of those black people could vote.

In the summer of 1964, the Student Nonviolent Coordinating Committee (SNCC, pronounced "snick") launched a full-scale campaign to register black voters in Mississippi. SNCC hoped to build a new political force in the state, the Mississippi Freedom Democratic Party (MFDP). To aid in the work, SNCC recruited students from Stanford, Yale, and other prestigious northern universities. Some eight hundred young men and women volunteered to go to Mississippi for "Freedom Summer."

One of the first volunteers to reach Mississippi was Andrew Goodman, a twenty-year-old white student from Queens College in New York. On his first morning, he set out to investigate the burning of a black church near the Mississippi town of Philadelphia. With him were two experienced civil-rights workers, both in their early twenties: Michael Schwerner, a white man from Brooklyn; and James Chaney, a black Mississippian.

That evening, the three young men failed to call in to SNCC headquarters. Fearing the worst, SNCC notified the local police and the FBI. Deputy Sheriff Cecil Price of Philadelphia admitted that he had arrested the three men that afternoon, allegedly for speeding. Price claimed they had been released within a few hours. But no one knew where they were now.

The disappearance of Chaney, Schwerner, and Goodman received enormous attention from the media. The FBI mounted an all-out search. As agents dragged the swamps and combed the

Michael Schwerner, Andrew Goodman, and James Chaney

woods, they uncovered one decaying body after another. They were the remains of black people, nameless and forgotten, who had been killed and buried by unknown hands. "It's tragic," said Rita Schwerner, Michael Schwerner's wife, "that white northerners have to be caught up in the machinery of injustice and indifference in the South before the American people register concern."

On August 4, an FBI team found the bodies of Goodman, Schwerner, and Chaney inside a recently built dam on a farm near Philadelphia. Twenty-one men were arrested in the case, including Sheriff Price. But the state dropped all charges against them. Six of the accused finally served prison time for violating federal civil-rights statutes.

Nearly eighty thousand black men and women registered with the MFDP during the summer of 1964. An MFDP contingent attended the Democratic National Convention in Atlantic City, New Jersey, and two MFDP representatives were seated as part of the Mississippi delegation. It was a small but crucial crack in the white power structure.

Freedom Summer had a profound impact on everyone who took part. "The poverty and sorrow of the neighborhoods doesn't leave you," one white freedom rider wrote to his parents. "I've seen the hands of these people, swollen and bruised, hard and calloused from years of work at practically no pay . . . and I realize very suddenly and forcefully that these are my people, and their sorrow is mine also, and our grief is collective, whether the rest of the country admits it or not."

Freedom Summer transformed the lives of thousands of black people as well. Fannie Lou Hamer, the wife of a sharecropper, became an eloquent leader in the MFDP. "After the project when all of the young people came down for the summer . . . Negro people in the Delta began moving," she told an interviewer years later. "People who had never before tried, though they'd always been anxious to do something, began moving!"

On July 2, 1964, President Lyndon B. Johnson signed a civil-rights act that banned all forms of discrimination on the basis of a person's color, ethnic origin, gender, or religion. It was the most important piece of civil-rights legislation passed since the end of the Civil War. Yet the fight was

President Johnson shakes hands with Martin Luther King, Jr., after signing the Civil Rights Act of 1964.

far from over. Complicated registration procedures still deliberately kept most African Americans from voting in the South. To demand the constitutional right to vote, the Southern Christian Leadership Conference (SCLC), led by Dr. King, planned a march from Selma, Alabama, to the state capitol in Montgomery.

On Sunday, March 7, 1965, six hundred men, women, and children marched through the streets of Selma. Their voices lifted in the songs that inspired the movement: "We Shall Overcome," and "Oh, Freedom!" But as they crossed the bridge leading out of the city, mounted Alabama state troopers ordered them to halt. The marchers knelt on the bridge and

On March 7, 1965, Alabama state troopers used tear gas and clubs to stop demonstrators who planned to march from Selma to Montgomery to protest voting discrimination.

On March, 9, the demonstrators made another attempt to march to Montgomery, but again were turned back by state troopers.

refused to move. After two minutes, the police attacked. Swinging billy clubs and firing tear gas, they charged on horseback into the unarmed crowd.

People scattered in terror. One of the fleeing marchers was an eight-year-old girl named Sheyann Webb. "I saw people being beaten, and I tried to run home as fast as I could," she explained later. "And as I began to run home I saw horses behind me. [An SCLC leader] picked me up, and I told him to put me down, he wasn't running fast enough!"

That evening, the whole bloody scene aired on television in millions of American homes. "It looked like war," admitted Selma mayor Joseph Smitherman. "It went all over the country. And the wrath of the nation came down on us."

On March 21, after a judge upheld their right to march, Martin Luther King and thousands of supporters were finally able to begin the five-day march from Selma to Montgomery without interference from Alabama police.

After the attack on the bridge, some African Americans argued that it was time to meet force with force. But King and other leaders still believed unshakeably in nonviolence. In the days after "Bloody Sunday," they calmed the crowds and laid plans for another peaceful march. This time, there would be no bloodshed. The president and the attorney general promised that the marchers would have the protection of hundreds of army troops, FBI agents, and federal marshalls.

On March 21, a vast column of marchers set out from Selma, singing songs of freedom. One of the marchers was John Lewis, who had been on the disastrous freedom ride to New Orleans four years before. "You didn't get tired," he recalled. "You had to go. It was more than an ordinary march for me. There was never a march like this one before. There hasn't been one since."

After five days on the road, the marchers reached Montgomery. By now, their ranks had swelled to 25,000. Dr. King spoke from the steps of the Alabama State Capitol. His voice rolled out over the listening crowd, predicting a day when America would be "a society at peace with itself, a society that can live with its conscience."

Dr. King speaking in front of the Alabama State Capitol after the completion of the march on March 25, 1965

People waiting to register to vote in Selma, Alabama, in 1965

On August 6, 1965, President Johnson signed a
ground-breaking piece of legislation that struck
down literacy tests and all other barriers that
denied the vote to African Americans. "The vote
is the most powerful instrument ever devised by
man for breaking down injustice," he said from
the United States Capitol. "The Voting Rights Act
is one of the most monumental laws in the entire
history of American freedom."

For her ninth birthday, Sheyann Webb asked
her parents to register to vote. They took her with
them the first time they went to the polls. "I will
never forget it," she said in an interview years
later. "You know, what even made it so unique to

me was the fact of it being so simple, just a check on the ballot at that particular time. . . . It was very exciting. It was exciting to them to have that right, as well as for me to see them do it."

African Americans had finally won a constitutional right that most Americans had long taken for granted. At last they were free to participate in the political process, to help choose officials who would represent their interests. The era of the freedom riders gave African Americans a voice, a voice that would never be silenced again.

African Americans voting in a primary election in Alabama in 1966

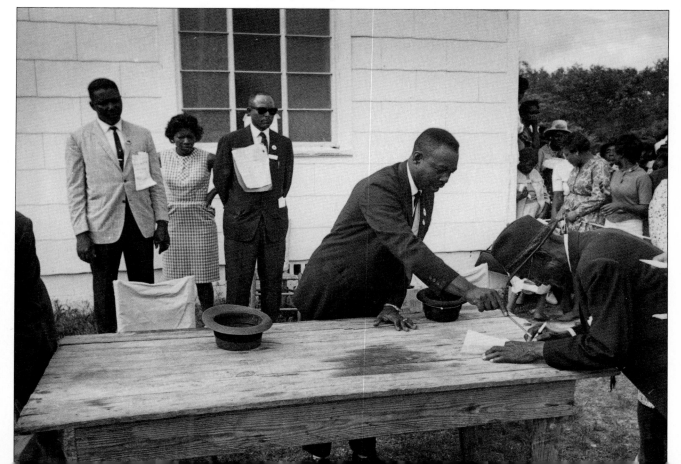

INDEX

PHOTO CREDITS

Cover, 1, 2, AP/Wide World; 3, 4, Historical Pictures/Stock Montage; 5, 6, 7, 8, 9 (both photos), 10, 11, 12, 13 (both photos), 14, 15 (both photos), 16, AP/Wide World; 17, Historical Pictures/Stock Montage; 18 (both photos), 19, 20, AP/Wide World; 21, North Wind Picture Archives; 23 (all three photos), 24, AP/Wide World; 25, 26, 27, 28, 29, 30, UPI/Bettmann; 31, AP/Wide World

Picture Identifications:
Cover: Black and white passengers sit side by side on a Norfolk, Virginia, bus the day after the Supreme Court handed down a decision banning segregation on interstate transportation.
Page 1: The freedom-rider bus that was set on fire outside Anniston, Alabama
Page 2: Martin Luther King, Jr., shaking hands with a freedom rider in Montgomery, Alabama

Project Editor: Shari Joffe
Designer: Karen Yops
Photo Editor: Jan Izzo
Cornerstones of Freedom Logo: David Cunningham

ABOUT THE AUTHOR

Deborah Kent grew up in Little Falls, New Jersey, and received her B.A. from Oberlin College. She earned a master's degree in social work from Smith College, and worked for four years at the University Settlement House on New York's Lower East Side.

Ms. Kent left social work to begin a career in writing. She published her first novel, *Belonging,* while living in San Miguel de Allende, Mexico. She has written a dozen novels for young adults, as well as numerous nonfiction titles for children. She lives in Chicago with her husband and their daughter Janna.